Joyflight

Cate Kennedy

Interactive Press
Brisbane

Interactive Press
an imprint of Interactive Publications
Treetop Studio • 9 Kuhler Court
Carindale, Queensland, Australia 4152
sales@ipoz.biz
www.ipoz.biz/ip/ip.htm

First published by Interactive Press, 2004

Printed in 12 pt Cochin on 14 pt Cochin by Imprint, Queensland, Australia.
Made, printed and bound in Australia.

National Library of Australia
Cataloguing-in-Publication data:

Kennedy, Cate, 1963- .
Joyflight.

ISBN 1 876819 26 X.

I. Title. (Series: Emerging authors series (Carindale, Queensland))

A821.4

Interactive Press

Joyflight

Cate Kennedy's first collection of poetry, **Signs of Other Fires** (Five Islands Press, 2001), was Highly Commended in the Victorian Premier's Awards, and won the Vincent Buckley Poetry Prize in 2002, allowing her to travel to Ireland where many of the poems in this second collection were written or inspired.

She has had poetry published in Cordite, the Newcastle Poetry Anthology, Blast and the Journal of Australian Studies, and broadcast on ABC Radio National. She has also won several national prizes for short fiction.

Joyflight was joint winner of the 2004 IP Picks national poetry award, with Nora Krouk's Skin for Comfort. In their report, the judges described the manuscript as 'a collection of poems dedicated to exploring the moment and rich with the details of life. Cate Kennedy is an intelligent poet with a remarkable ability to freshen the language. In **Joyflight**, Kennedy gets inside her subjects and helps us to view the world from unique and different perspectives.'

Cate Kennedy teaches creative writing, especially the short story form, and lives on a farm on the Broken River in northeast Victoria.

The Emerging Authors Series showcases the best new Australian literary talent and is available in digital and print form.

for my father

We have to disappear into the midst of those we don't know, so they will suddenly pick up something of ours from the street, from the sand, from the leaves that have fallen for a thousand years in the same forest…and will take up gently the object we have made…In that object, poetry will live…

– Pablo Neruda, *Memoirs*

Acknowledgements

Cover design: David Reiter
Author photos: Ursula Read

My thanks to the Australian Centre at the University of Melbourne, and Penelope Buckley, for the Vincent Buckley Award, which allowed me to travel in Ireland in 2002. I am also grateful to the Australia Council for providing me with a New Works grant in 2002, which allowed me to dedicate more time to poetry, and to Ron Pretty, who has given me, and so many other writers, his encouragement and support. Thanks to Sara Moss, for the editor's gift of labouring to clarify someone else's thoughts. And last of all heartfelt thanks to David Dore, best companion after a solitary day.

"Five Encounters with Birds" was included in the 2003 Newcastle Poetry Anthology CD. "Following the Game" was published by *Cordite* online magazine in 2003. "Forgetting the Language" appeared in *Wild About the Roof,* the Wollongong Poetry Workshop Anthology 2001, published by Five Islands Press. "This Is Summer" appeared in the *Journal of Australian Studies* anthology no. 73: *The Dog of War,* in 2002.

Contents

Joyflight

That pure torn-open moment

I am leaving this house at the base of a mined hill.
Walk up there and see poisoned subsoil
turned upside-down 120 years ago,
laced with cyanide, sunk into dark cave-ins –
nothing native ever finds a hold again
bramble and gorse sprawl snarling over the clay
glinting pale like a scar through hair.

You told me to keep the table,
its legs drilled with the holes of borers.
This is just the kind of timber they like –
milled and stained,
resembling hardwood.
Do you remember how we tried treating it for a while,
injecting kerosene with a syringe?
I see us there, on our knees together
our fingertips searching out holes like braille
back before we lost interest in preservation.

Nocturnal, voracious, they go in
like a self-tapping screw.
In the morning we'd find tiny piles of sawdust on the floor
sifted into gold dust pyramids,
sweep them up like tailings.

They've worked the table over
they've done it in
it lists now, drilled into its core
rocks under the flat of my hands
ready, like an old slipping dislocation,
to give way
under a palm's insistent pressure.

I keep pausing in my packing, here alone in the house
to walk outside and look at the hill
its bitter prickling greens and exposed sediments.
Locals say never to walk through the old mines and mullock heaps alone;
riddled with subsidence, the old fortifications rotted,
it's impossible to guess when a still-treacherous cavity
might suddenly
open up, out of nowhere
finally exhausted
with the duty of disguising
such eroded and abandoned visions.

This morning they yarded the weaner calves.
All day they've been bawling
in the bitter cold

shuffling together and crying out
in the absence of their mothers
tracking up and down the wire fence

it's like they keep forgetting
so the separation strikes them afresh
every little while

they're choked with snot
hoarse, plaintive, thirsty;
water won't do it
they want milk.

I put on talkback radio
to drown out their wails
but that's a mistake.

It's a litany of grievance
the weaners
are only learning what we all have to learn –

to live without it
to keep pressing along those fences
to keep forgetting why.

My father's stories
must be provoked from him
by some landslide of sorrow;
a lost city's foundations revealed by shifting earth.
Only after the death of two brothers
does he relate some childhood moment
of a Sunday after Mass, when a Tiger Moth
touched down on a patch of ground
offering joy flights.

I see them, those three blonde boys taut with longing
that silver machine, the sky.
My father remembers the sum of money required for the three boys to go up
and his own father's face, closed and abashed, after he asked the pilot.
He turned away
my father steeled himself for the walk home to lunch.
Yet somehow his father was carrying the money, and somehow he decided.
They flew.

Disaster could have struck, and sent my grandmother mad with grief.
My grandfather would have been condemned
to watch that, from the ground, forever.
But nothing went wrong.
They flew, and returned safely to the earth, transformed,
an awestruck moment in a poor childhood,
desire made real, a stern father hiding his smile on the run home.

Everyone but my father who witnessed that event is dead now.
He hands me the story, a small recovered legacy,
glinting and bright with disuse.
Now I carry those three buffeted grinning children in their Sunday clothes
hardly able to believe their luck,
astonished by joy and flight.

I hold this, and yearn to write fiction
in the face of these deaths and losses,
in the face of all that is forgotten
and revealed by the stark shift of pain and surprise.
I want to carry this talisman carved like a rune
for my father, for my uncles, for my grandfather, and for that pilot;
for that pure torn-open moment
where they each slipped free of the earth.
Fiction, which is the ribbon pulled from a trembling mouth,
which tells its truth with such defiance
that everything forgotten will blaze, every joy burnished
every recollection of unexpected flight shared
and passed from hand to cupped hand,
carried warm next to the skin,
recited for courage.

July 15th, 1975 – The Apollo-Soyuz Link-Up

We're fixated on payload down here –
breeding anthrax and ebola in the ice-age of cold wars.
The two supernations have sent up spacecraft like defiant banners
circling in the black, blank tundra of space.
On July 15th, the cosmonauts discard Einstein's notes on atomic theory
for those less-plundered, less-understood pages on time and place.

In space, even machinery touches with the grace of a boat
hatch to hatch, the doorways align, and metal smelted in an enemy zone
in forges on both sides of the planetary garrison cross the moat
they grate in silence then hold
like two pieces of the Rosetta Stone.

Airlocked. Both are bolted fast.
Then one crew of cosmonauts steps into no-man's land.
Their crafts lie welded like insects mated in an empty black vault of vast
and airless dark. The clocks slow
and we, landlocked by so much gravity,
we watch them coupled through the monitor's faulty, blinding snow.

We wait, squinting at the smoking field,
the rubble of countdown-warfare in the sucking mud.
We are all holding vats of oil and meaningless
treaty documents, bibles, vials, a flood
of mutating cultures, grenades –
it is a tricky business, weightlessness.

The Russians step through, floating, to greet
the white-flag smile of the Stars and Stripes.
The crews visit one another in the inky neutral vacuum of sky.
War docks a moment.
They talk, we are suddenly certain,
about the massive blue-green meniscus below

that watching eye
beloved and coming into view
through the starboard porthole.
We all orbit, staring up breathless, amazed
mouths open, euphoric
shell-shocked, dazed.

Even on the conveyor belt, the men pause to clench and swallow
each state-of-the-art anti-personnel mine
for a moment stays disassembled
in harmless bits of springs and cogs and wires.
Over the mud trenches we come, limping,
through corpses and fires.
"Silent Night" we sing in our fierce ache for home,
each language in that chorus
transposes with the others.

For five minutes in July 1975,
it's Christmas, midnight, 1916, in Passchendaele
our heads tilt up at that bright candle in space
We rise from the murky bunkers blind, our fingers splayed
to read that strange constellation like braille.

The centre's deadening pull slips somehow
some heavy locked door falters on its hinges, slides ajar –
for a moment it all seems as possible
and miraculous as a star.

A trip to the city. A family wanders past the floral clock
when a light rain
drives them inside the art gallery.

Her sister wants to look at the stained glass windows in the foyer
and run her fingers along the mesmerising water
streaming down the plate glass.
Her mother browses in the foyer shop for gift cards.
Desultory, they follow the crowds through the exhibit doors
filling in time until the weather clears.

In the first gallery they come across a retrospective of drawings
by Picasso, recently dead and deified,
the dizzying output of a loose, utterly confident pencil.
Her mother whispers to her father that they hardly seem worth framing.
The child stares through the shifting bodies of milling adults
at Picasso's portrait of a young woman.

As her family makes a cursory circuit around the bulls and battles
she looks at the eyes, the two u-shapes making irises
the five eyelashes stalks of crayon, pure and precise,
the mouth swept in a bow in four strokes
the whole face a single flourish of careless joy.

Something closes in her throat, then opens.
A hand somewhere
sweeps a piercing, unerring line through her chest.

The rain has stopped.
Her sister and parents return, promising a visit to the donut van
before they go to the car.
As they walk out she cannot name the change, the dislocation.
It is as if the lozenges of light in those foyer windows

have been reassembled, the blood beats in her head
as though newly transfused, these people strangers
speaking a dulled and muffled language.

Those eyes under their winged brows, grave and perfect,
watch everything with their luminous compassion.
They have seen before what they see now;
a child, suddenly subdued,
something inside swept raw and newly secretive
judging now, silently
what must be kept hidden to survive;
the vigilant camouflage of thorn bushes
the grim survey lines of loneliness it will require.

lime cordial summers
the telly murmured three day tests
in the only room with a fan

we would end up there, collapsed
in cut-off jeans
stupefied
with the white lethargy of school holidays

we lay loose-limbed and aching with the wait
Colombo's sunshine looked like chrome
the players moved sluggish
in the tropical heat
roused themselves again
and again to run

sweat
trickled down our adolescent cleavage
as we watched, sucking ice cubes,
the fan's face a mechanical, slow-motion negation

the ball clocked gently
so much molten time
that rhythmic, momentary taste
of moving air

we wanted the burning vinyl of bench seats
boys who smelled of petrol
a cool change, quickening pulses
wanted a roar, wickets flying, limbs
taut with anticipation

total fire ban, day after day
the hot concrete

stretched like a glaring empty pitch to the Hill's Hoist
those storm clouds massed
waiting for release
the supporters' slow clap
building, poised:
thunder
a drum roll
elsewhere

1

Struck by the car, a misjudged airlift
the gravel edge yawning beyond the tyre
impact pulls it up over the bonnet
and it drags slowly across the windscreen
splayed dislocated wing up in a gesture
which cups the slipstream, a thirsty palm in a hard current
the perfect useless spread of those feathers
like a hand of black and white cards
head a blown egg
and the neck
pivoted off its axis now
bone a snapped and unmendable spring come loose

stretched back, as past caring as a drowned Ophelia
throat exposed beyond possibility
the beak describes the curved arc of wiper blade
with sumptuous disdain
and is lipped up and tossed away
it is four seconds
of stillness, flattened by wind on to a screen
a glimpsed secret passage
from violence, panic, this life,
into the elongated calm of release
the glass and pressure
a brief delay before disconnection
breaking the measured slide between here and there
and what I see are those two dark claws –
ten seconds ago hesitating, flexed over hot tarmac –
stretching lazily,
then closing around themselves, finished
like two blackened fronds of fern.

2

On the road between Celaya and Queretaro, Mexico
on a crossroad ringed by speed humps,
where all traffic
must pass slowed to a crawl
lies glittering tarmac and flat dazzle of monoxide heat.
Human figures traverse the intersection,
selling to a captive audience of stalled vehicles
car stickers and seat covers, potato chips and warm Fanta
cooking pots glazed with lead
lottery tickets, novelties.
This is a landscape stretched flat and panting
with the assault of plunder –
cactus wrenching itself over rubble,
dust storms rising off soil pumped with agrophosphates,
the distant toxic shimmer of sweatshops in the next town.

Everything has been spent, free-traded, fire-saled
cornfields ploughed under for carnations
batteries for chickens, pigs and humans
constructed from cement block
and pushed to the edge of the map like flotsam.
We beckon over the hawkers with the drinks and snacks
in a lead-fuel shimmer of inertia.
One vendor stands next to the speed hump motionless
holding out a stick
roosting on its end is an owl.
All is distilled into an abject vortex
around this small bird
brinked and wired there.
It clutches, hunched and sick,
a desperate remnant wild envoy
from a desert country running out of things to sell
eating the lesson of market forces like dust.
It waits like a rock for this to be over
expiring in incremental heartbeats, staring at the dust
from the end of the stick

dreamy with forgotten life – two eggs somewhere
are rotting in a tree still left standing
waiting for a machete
to feed the kilns to fire the pots
being carried from car to car.
Its beak is buried in its chest, head bowed,
its captor praying for someone, inconceivably,
with pity and money for an owl, for the shame
to reduce itself to a transaction,
for something to happen
before death makes everything worthless.
I saw a child like this once for sale, in Pattaya, Thailand
standing with the same patience
outside a bar on the prostitutes' strip
She stood
gazing at the ground, hands resting on thighs
fingers folded and touching like tucked wings
the head and shoulders too big for a body
designed for anything
except this offering up.

3

Now I have a season watching swans – a pair on a lake
tending their diminishing family.
Ten weeks ago they emerged bowing from the rushes
with eight floating grey balls of down,
single perfect sneezes,
the black molten-glass necks of the adults
dipped and curved around the flock.
Three weeks later five remained –
the others drowned, frozen or lost.
At five weeks, the cygnets staggered ashore,
their necks stretching, feathers growing in,
the parent birds facing intruders
making sounds like a stick hitting a fence.
The big male meant business – feathers up like hackles,
clumsy and menacing as a heavyweight.

Four cygnets, three.
The adults' wings, out on the water, unfolded
with a shock of white strength like kites caught in a gust
you could hear the bones beat the water.
At night, out there in the rushes
came gargling cries of distress,
the moony, slavering yowl of foxes,
then nothing.
It's like this every year,
as the earth warms and children throw bread,
the same pair, that sound which scares nobody,
the aching lines of the throat, the cold fog rising
and the gradual cull.
Then one morning, there are two left.
They are surrounded by dense silence.
The parents raise their heads out of mist as I approach
the male jerks his defiant dance
their eyes are so red
and so clear that I tremble.

4

Sometimes, like this, there is a quick rupture
between their world and ours
a pigeon falling down the chimney upstairs
into a workroom full of drawings
hitting the hearth in a thump of coaldust which rises
in a slow and voluptuous cloud to settle,
fine as talcum, over every surface.
No human is there to witness the bird's purposeful tramp
over the tabletops,
stumbling into a saucer of water first,
so that its feet pick out smeared tracks across each sketch
its tail and wings redistributing charcoal
blurring outlines
marking black paths across those reclining nudes.
It is like dusting for prints to follow its progress:
pecking at pastels, blinking black dust from its eyes.

Before I find and release it I imagine it turning back
to consider the ways it has come,
baffled in this confined alternate universe
traversing and retraversing,
feet and body encrusted with the irrefutable evidence
of circumnavigation.
Later, I see it in a nearby park.
Identical to the other pigeons
save for the streaks of charcoal,
it rests beneath the outstretched hand of a statue.
As it settles there that stone gesture seems to melt
from the wary open confusion of an English explorer, feigning confidence
to fingers curled to touch something palpably within reach
a hand that could be feeling for a quill
or offering a grave benediction.
For a moment, as the bird shifts, this is a hand
that has discarded its rolled-up map, its gripped sexton
and is poised now, it seems,
to smooth those smeared feathers
or to close calmly on nothing but air.

5

Then this morning one last messenger, a spotted turtledove
swoops through the back door into the darkness of the house
the haphazard urban backyard
turns sharply into blind quest
these dim-lit corridors become blundering traps
that small heart almost stops.
I find it beating against a window
wings scrabbling like apologetic fingertips
turned mindless with the newly-treacherous universe
gasping for unreachable sky.
In my hands its wings hunch forward
into the shrug of the starving.

I am holding a light fistful of hollow bones,
a thin feathered pocket of airborne hooks,
a fragile-crumpled hat,
the second day of Christmas stored tissue-wrapped in a box.
Its head lies against my palm in a serpentine curve,
surrendered, landlocked, and still.
Here this is a pest species, as invasive as rats, everywhere
yet that miraculous plumage,
those spots lapping the neck,
that violet sheen
stops me in my tracks at the door.
Sensing light and air currents, it convulses in my grasp
as if touched with a charged wire.

Is time as fluid as this to a flight animal?
Years or moments spent poised like this, stilled
then galvanising into one thin silver line of escape
within seconds, something lost
lies now behind these devious clear panes
writhing free, that small eye
holds an elliptical expanse of sky
like a single tear.

These birds, and the million others
tilting through lengthening dusk
in the decreasing spaces, in dwindling free air
struggling across oceans, claw-scratching at our memories
those tiny collisions
with our glazed right-angled surfaces
shock a tiny gentleness from us
eggshell-thin, our fragile pity
jolts a circuit like a glimpse of open sky
our shoulders twist
our fingers hover, not wanting to touch
yet still weaving themselves, helpless,
into nests.

Leonardo said it
paint blue sky five times darker
the five times farther you wish it to appear

grinding cobalt and linseed
wasting painting time
coming up with equations
I see a studio of copyists
refining the buttermilk complexion
of La Giaconda
those dense oils
dust motes
saturated silence

and the master
who had flayed open every sinew
of cadavers for inspection
from whom no secret was sacrosanct
who stared each dead pauper in the eye
kept his gaze on the horizon
considering craft designed to rise
and enter that darkening atmosphere
while his left hand, second-guessing us,
scratched instructions
backwards

I've been sent a postcard from Canada
of an Eskimo building an igloo from within
he reaches upwards in grey frostbite light
towards a rough disk of blue

that's all I hear from you;
no chinks for wind or ice,
no word of northern sky –
your black silhouette
bulky with new layers
your face turned away

suspended here in this polar blind drift
I watch speechless as you cut frozen bricks
to make hostility into a home

what I need to know
is eighty different words for snow.

We wake to screaming hoarse noise,
the old bull
trampling through a fence
has attacked the young bull.
The object of their battle, the cows,
huddle together uneasy
in a far corner away from the arena.

It takes dogs and a vehicle to separate them;
the old bull bruised and limping, enraged and abusive
forced back to his lonely paddock
his usurper – younger, a weight advantage, on top of his form
better at disguising his damage
calls back *any time, old man*
and shoulders his way back to prime position under a tree.

All day the old bull moans unspeakable injustice
restates his case
screams up and down the boundary
limping on his bleeding hoof
making a show of resenting the fence.
The cows eye him –
girlfriends after a pub brawl –
flattered, but unmoved.

Now he stands with his back to the lot of them
staring into the distance, sentinel to his own silence.
He shifts his weight on sore legs,
remnant power
rippling through his shoulders,
throat raw with threat
righteous as an old gladiator,
his raised chin
a profile for a coin.
There is dust coating the slobber drooled down his chest
and nothing on the horizon
to warrant his pose of steely resolve.
He won't lie down
until it's dark.

honeymoon
makes a mockery
of rock and dust
this surface is white
but warm
your fingers plant a flag
on the lunar curve of my belly
the moon's light rains silver
on the sharp eclipse of your shoulder
the waves, dreaming, turn and exhale
like a glittering curtain, opening, closing, opening
name me
I am an orb
of nectar

A hot bath of river water, tinged like weak tea
I lie washed and boneless
staring at a poster on the bathroom wall –
THE SOUTHERN CROSS AND THE POINTERS –
thinking of you
suspended, amniotic, lapped
and your sudden death

that green plastic kidney dish and the smell
of my own blood like earth clinging to an uprooted tree.

My husband drew me this bath
your father
who wept tears I'd never witnessed
as your sanctuary bled from me
who wants me to relax.
I hate every period pain
every unmistakable precursor
sharpening into cramp this month.

My head rests on the rim
detached from my failed body;
my pelvic bones,
cupping nothing,
rise like empty islands.

Was it something unaligned,
a flawed compass reading,
a co-ordinate that lost us?
the week you developed fingerprints
placenta bright as sun behind eyelids
you were mis-carried,
ill-conceived.

Hospital staff found a vein in me
to replenish every saline trembling drop
as if it was water I'd lost.

The moon waxes
and nothing fuses in the darkness
in this body edgy with scoured nerves
weightless in warm water, in my husband's childhood house.
You orbit now beyond my gravity.
I am without instruments, an abandoned craft
bereft of my best idea.
Show me what star will guide me now
what constellation.

What heat hatches is parasites
they arrive
urgent as a contraction
scenting blood, sweat, rot, sap
their bodies bite like threaded screws into new wood
all mouth, they clamp up trunks, skeletonise leaves
mass in water to set up home in the gut

hold your hand in the grass
lower your face inch by inch to the ground,
settle in the path of five billion consumers
just under your massive surface, scented, assessed, tapped
pulse fuel resources
if you just lay there
surrendered,
you would be so efficiently dismantled,
broken down into salts and sugars
your glazed irises sipped delicately by ants
if you still stared, unblinking
flowering weeds would spurt through the sockets
your greenhouse ribs would be twined
with the voracious red tongues of blackberry vines
larvae would tread the neatly-ploughed fields of your fingerprints,
eyeless, ruthless, perfect
it is all perfect – it is stupefying
it is never finished

this is Summer, this universe in an inch of stagnant water, this
spawning of glossy rats under the pine needles
and, packed like worshippers up the stalk
the luxuriant green bloom of translucent aphids
unhurriedly drinking a rose to death.

There is a rat setting up residence
in the hinged hollow bench seat
we store the recycled wrapping paper in

I hear it shuffling and gnawing in there
wearing down those yellow teeth
that never stop growing.

It's not the trapping and killing I mind.
Not even the lethal 3 a.m. deathsnap
and that indrawn 10 seconds like fingernails on the blackboard

the muffled writhing slalom like a hooked flathead
and the noise like steam escaping a kettle
all idea of silence and secrecy gone.

I understand a broken neck
will never be quiet or orderly, that death
probably comes, as they assure me, in the first instant.

Even removing the body is OK – by the morning
lifeless as a discarded glove puppet
stiff and huddled, easy to avert your eyes from.

It's lifting the hinge on that seat to inspect the damage
seeing what's attracted it
excavating what's stored there to find what it's eaten through

the paper that wrapped gifts that came with bereavement cards
florists' paper, tissue and ribbon, barely creased
all the giftwrap saved from last year's numb Christmas

those folded and well-meant condolences, smoothed flat
and blindly stowed with autopilot hands, for some unthinkable time
when new presents and bouquets of flowers might require them

that billow of rat heat, clumped fur and spit as you lift the lid
intimate, secretive, cellulose pulp chewed and nosed through
shredded for a nest – this is what turns your stomach,

having to peel each of those interred layers away, the churning thought
of some parasite seeing it all as food
and worse, somewhere to hole up; somewhere warm and desirable to live.

I no longer have the heart for this painstaking archaeology.
Give me the sudden fizzing agony, then nothing
I'd take the trap any day.

Before we fitted the window, the mudwasps came
as they had for years,
and made a bulbous nest on the brick wall.

All through the fitting of ceiling rafters and roof I watched them,
striped and gleaming like poisonous sweets, legs dangling
droning in and out of the wall cavity with their wet balls of mud,
patting it layer by scrupulous layer into a nest.

Those busy, impossible abdomens,
connected with a fine-threaded needle to thorax,
curved over as they worked.
The framing finished, the newly-glazed window
sealed and fitted, showed us sky and river
contained like a postcard.

It is our territory now, lined with bookshelves and carpet,
and the nest has stayed there, sequestered, all through winter
swelling unnoticed high up against the bricks.
Seven months have passed, and now wasps
are hitting against the glass outside, feeling around
this barrier to their remembered flight path.
Two wasps have blundered through the house
incongruous as helicopters,
clawing hunched at closed windows everywhere.

In the mud nest
two perfectly round holes.

I hesitate, here with my kitchen knife and dustpan
frightened of what lies walled up in there
something cramped and fully-grown
waiting to be released
winged and barbed and shining like armour
and still, outside the window,
that insistent knocking,
come to claim what is theirs

After the competition closed
the organisers ran a short column in their newsletter
explaining that, much to their dismay
and due to circumstances
completely beyond their control
their post-office box had been broken open and some entries stolen
by someone clearly searching for cheques.
Arriving at the scene, they had found
torn poems
and crumpled empty envelopes
strewn in the gutter nearby.
They apologised, urging last-minute entrants to resubmit.

This is the fraught journey of language;
words blind and curled
ruptured from folded clean darkness and into the glare,
blown down streets, into stormwater drains, lost at sea
composted, clipped by traffic, stillborn,
a message without a stamp
half a love sonnet bleeding like a bitten tongue.

This is the risk, this ungainly and defenceless sprawl
into a world that frowns upon litter
harsh hands intent on finding some other, more recognisable currency
to feed some other, more pressing addiction.

The organisers apologise
but are helpless in the face of this short-circuit.
We stand and survey this hotwired wreckage
the lock broken,
the door swinging useless on a torn hinge,
and an exploded safe of words
adrift and on their way, uncancelled and unchartered

chaotic as discarded betting slips
confetti at the world's wedding
rained-on hieroglyphs from elsewhere

eroding gently
they wait, like an unlit fuse, to be decoded
by the unsuspecting anthropologist
emerging now, on cue, from a doorway up the road.
They think they're going out for a coffee
if they only knew
they are on a collision course
with scattered blossom.

Burning the world's almanac

In 1849 a group of 150 famine victims were denied sustenance at the poorhouse in Westport, County Mayo, Ireland, until they had registered with the so-called "Poor Commissioners", based 14 miles away at Delphi House. In the depths of winter they walked there through the valley by Croagh Patrick, Ireland's Holy Mountain, only to find that the commissioners were having dinner and would not see them. Dozens froze to death in the snow. A stone monument on the place today reads: To COMMEMORATE THE HUNGRY POOR WHO WALKED HERE IN 1849, AND WALK THE THIRD WORLD TODAY.

And what were they thinking, finally, as they sank down,
hope extinguished,
or was it a relief to stop thinking
only reeling, drifting in and out in the whirling sleet
glimpsing your father there, huddled, vanishing
so that the snow at last
a misjudged enemy
invited you down to rest,
muffling each voice
and a faint half-dreamed comfort
in closing your eyes on your knees in the shadow of the Croagh
named for the saint who fasted,
like Our Saviour,
only both from choice.

Beyond bitter curses, then, or did they die raging,
snot and tears freezing on their faces?
Who was chosen to muster
a semblance of dignity
to approach the house,
and how to return
to break the news to the others,
and with what words?

And the men in the house, never dreaming
that this would be the moment seized by fate
to expose them
this, which was commonplace, no doubt;
they were Commissioners, only that, righteous with due process,
stamps and nibs put away for the day, and now
dealing with a nuisance, irritable,
pushing the last of the bread
around their plate.

Would they have behaved better
if they knew they were to be judged
jump to stoke the fire,
order a tureen of soup made,
swing open those doors,
be exemplary?
History catches us like this,
buttons undone and disguises off
aggrieved with burdensome paperwork
maintaining order in some godforsaken outpost
and, frankly, the poor always with us

and so these hundred and fifty,
unnamed,
condemned to white oblivion
by a flat refusal,
one stone, now, suffices for them all.

It is the past we find containable
folded along old certainties
like a map or a card
a stone to mark distance,
reduced to well-worn lines,
observed through a square glass pane:
the Hungry Poor, outside the gates at Delphi House
the villains and the victims
the snow soaked with amnesia,

frozen here and rendered into monochrome
by this driving rain

but they are with us
trudging with the last of their energy,
thousands of miles now, from poorhouses and famine fields
chilled and exiled,
holding pitchforks or children or unsigned paperwork,
forged, faded identifications,
the wrong currencies,
they are with us and we will not see them
as they come through the valley
spurred by a mirage of lit windows
and laughable hopes of some borrowed hearth,
they are with us, and we are done with them
we will not meet their eye.

Tomorrow we will draw a red line in the ledger
pious and put-upon, holding this burden like a full plate
against our memory of thc cold

This is Delphi of the silenced, unrecognisable stones
Delphi where witness is a frozen and thawed and refrozen thing
Delphi, where the oracle speaks, and we do not listen.

The earth's crust is a theory of solidity:
in Chiapas once I stood on a shivering meniscus
the ground sustained a rolling tremor, twitched
like an animal's flank
I grabbed at air to keep
my footing, breathless
at this jarring revelation – the trembling skin beneath my feet
liquid as mercury, the grass
resettling like fur

Now this bog – dense and scored as book pages
moss mattress sinking like sponge
aerated with rot, springing
with compressed eons –
provides a notion of solid ground

We walk
on tectonic plates
fitted together like fontanel bones
this place here
is cartilage
saturated, flexing
I stand on this surface
an insect splayed on water's skin

What is history except fuel?
The locals watch as the tractors mash it to batter
extrude it into turf bricks
dislocate and reset the field
into bruised lines tagged for each buyer,
the smell as it burns
an incense of nostalgia.

There's nothing as sweet as that smell, they say
as tourists watch the hearth like television.
Something in our short lives –
the compression of memory, the careful stowing of every growth –
draws our cold fingers towards it in dreamy recognition;
we need that benign and blurring smoke
that crucible of glowing, exultant heat

In this silence I can hear it,
hissing and sighing
I am burning
the world's almanac

each notation
is a tiny tongue of expended warmth
unlocking small flurrying memories of cold
each death a curled, precise mark under a turned page
a pressed fern
a cycad

only moss
is what the peat confides
moss, moss and emptiness, it says,
hard winter, sun
green cold forever

Old Loreto Convent, Killarney

Wearing deprivation prickling next to the skin
they would have found this abandonment easier to bear
than any of us now, cosseted and over-tended by the world.
It is how they would have chosen it
to have the water close over their heads without struggle or regret,
ramrod straight, each identical black cross disappearing into weeds.

Rooks wheel a bickering chorus
harping over the same leaf-bare territories
above this walled enclosure choked with wild yarrow and dandelions.
All is silent now. None of them will tell a word of it.
They are elsewhere.

Rooks they were, too,
stalking down this path between the arthritic yews –
knife-sharp wind kiltering their habits sideways like black flapping kites –
to tend the graves of their sisters and clear the undisturbed spaces
of their own plots.
Here in this chill eyrie
their scrubbed knuckled hands gathering together
a steepling home threaded with sticks
this buffeted austere world nurturing none but themselves,
red-beaked and wary, huddled in the chapel's greyed nest.

It ended a lifetime's practice, fittingly,
to hammer flat each separate idiosyncrasy,
or what vestige could remain of it,
into these plain black crosses, gaunt and upright even now.
Only the brisk order: *pray for the soul of*
and the names and date of death lettered
bone-white face against the black adamant self-effacement
spiked in this forgotten field.

For all is relinquished in the end,
without adornment or achievement, without flowers;
the date you left this world
and the first name, the name that turned you
in the green and saturated orchard one day,
called you to this chapped humility
by a bleak mountain patterned with wind's shifting light
and the sunken earth plots of those gone before you,
let you glimpse this
and not turn your face away.

They are inches away
beneath my shoes
there would not be one
I would not tower over

here solidly astride
two feet planted in walking boots
upright, on calcium-rich bones
my long thighs straight as arrows
padded luxuriantly with flesh
my costly life
has brought me here, to them.

Such a waste
of muscle, sinew, dexterity
headfuls of teeth, hair, nails
language, thought, song scraps, lineage.
Lie them in a line,
let's get them limed and covered
before the snow sets in.

Now the grass rolls over them
grass they lay and tried to eat
when the last crop blackened and rotted
fingers knobbled with chilblains
scraping clear a trench.
These rubble walls were built by them.
Imagine this: to be paid in a cup of broth
to lift stones for walls
defining property boundaries for somebody else's land
that bore nothing but more starvation.

How could you take a pride in finishing
how could you, weakening, pick out just the stone
to fit, and take your hands away – there – and glance
up at the sky to wonder
what would endure here.

Not your own children, surely.
You must have watched them –
their blinking ponderous, coughs hacking, fitful –
wondering how and why you were allowed to bring them into this world
only for this
I imagine you doubted, then, what the priest told you
I imagine the soil broke easily under your spade.
So. In their clothes, hastily buried,
in scraps of hessian and wool, tied around with rags,
they lie within their own walls.

In five layers, myself, I complain of this cold
soon I'll be back in town, in time for lunch
to contemplate the million-dead-million-fled
and the nourishment, inconceivably,
it has required, to bring me here.

Great-great grandparents
all blood and bone now,
under this soil in a single green field
that will never again be cultivated.
I stand here uselessly muscled, sedentary,
sound, white, solid, surpassing all potential,
staring for so long that when I blink
red and white spots rush in front of my blue eyes like corpuscles.
Like Heaney I'm trying to hold this pen –
trying to direct this divining rod, quaking, towards paper
but it is a muddy fingerbone
prodding me to stand here, still;
again and again pointing down.

In a constant stream of pummelling Atlantic wind
after five minutes you walk like they did:
head down, armwrapped, tucked chin –
they set out in those oceans in *naimhóga*;
boats they made of lathed wood curved like a ribcage,
and stretched with skin.

They launched them from this stony beach
scrabbling for oars, into this plunging, icy shelf
their craft hit the water like something made of balsa
and past leather, wood, woollen clothes and the hot sheen of sweat
nothing but your chilled and naked self.

To eat, you faced that sea. The hull of your boat
light as a bough, sat low like two cupped hands
to be filled with mackerel.
Some years they ate seaweed and birds eggs, or lived on seal.
When the men could, they rowed to Mass on the mainland
as the Sacrament was raised
they held up a white sheet on the hilltop –
on the island, the women and old people, scanning the horizon
knew the moment to kneel.

They survived, or they died quietly.
Families launched their boats to fetch a coffin, then returned
grey with grief to take the body back to the churchyard in Dunquin.
There was a point down the cliffs;
Aitan Uaignis – the Place of Loneliness
where they would pause with their dead, panting,
then hoist the coffin again, to row them
three miles to the mainland, and consecrated ground.

Sometimes they waited there for days
left with nothing but the sound
of the sea moaning in the caves below
and a body in a box in the cold
waiting for the water to grow calm enough to make the crossing
and have this finished

How the world must have shrunk
with nothing left to distract you from what there was:
a blue-lipped wait in a corner of shelter
coins on the eyes
the smell of new timber shrinking, bleeding sap,
a boat made of skin
and gannets tumbling like Icarus
into that vast, indifferent sea.

The next bus noses around the stone walls shiny as a toy
its doors sigh open and release a load of grey tourists
blinking like rumpled sleepwalking children, ejected like larvae.
The driver has had them all day, at the feckin' castle,
and can hardly wait to be rid of them
he hurries into an adjoining bar
to get the taste of them out of his mouth with a Guinness

The mock-rustic pub is as deserted as a studio set after hours.
They step into dim emptiness –
a decorative gasfire burns ersatz blue flames in the grate
over fake nubs of varnished coal.
Behind the bar, an electric fan heater takes the edge off the cold.
The women arrange themselves, grinning self-consciously;
they are sitting in an Authentic Irish Pub
the men prowl with video cameras
sweeping the corners of the room like a forensics team
getting it all down.
The locals are home watching *Neighbours* and running B&Bs
they never come here now
sick of the live-to-air interviews and interminable family histories
being buttonholed by one of these big simple bores
at their old table in the corner.

It's drinks all round.
They sit, uncertain of the script
until a man with a piano accordion squares his shoulders,
walks as if towards a firing squad from the back room
and strikes up the blarney.
They know all the words to "Danny Boy".
The man's daughter leaves the TV somewhere
and skips out before them to do a Riverdance impression.
Every face beams behind its whirring electronic eye

every camera has a red-eye flash function
but when the girl turns away
her eyes are still hard as deflectors
something pulls the cord on her Disney smile
and she trudges back into the kitchen
to start microwaving their lasagne.

Sensing a possible moment of doubt
the man swings into "Irish Rover"
as his wife rubs something, hard, on the bar
with a chequered teatowel
and then turns away to balance the till.

This beach is a surfeit
the drenched stones sigh like a rapt audience
each one perfected
ribbed with quartz, or not
carved wet and waiting for a hand.

My lifetime
could produce one sanded as dense and skinsmooth as these
so to walk here, stung by chilled spray,
by persistent abradings,
is a lesson in small humilities.

It's not just me, dragging myself salt-scoured back to the car
with my pockets full,
arranging them in a line on the windowsill.
I pass houses miles away
where five or six calm masterpieces
are rolled to stillness in garden beds.
One porch inland has them laid up the steps to the door,
an altar to tide.

I will carry this one 7,000 miles
to the other tumbling edge of this same ocean,
stretched wrinkled across the blue globe
because I want to show you what made it irresistible;
its glistening settle as it clicked and nested on that beach,
that opalescent green storing an ocean's restless mouthings
as it lifts and arranges each stone into a single prayer.
I want to hold it still,
like a gull's egg,
warmed in my hands
waiting.

You planted them, so you know they're under there.
Find a soft spot. This could take half a day.
Then put your boot on the fork, and let it sink.

Choose a dry day, so that you won't wrench your back
turning soil heavy with water and risen clay.
The leaves and stalks will look finished,
black with early frost.
Do not be dissuaded: remember
the day you planted these
your attention seemed barely required;
donkey work – just dig a trench and cover them with straw –
but now they have shown you this strange reward for carelessness
when you turn your fork
they break the surface in clumps,
tumbling up from the dark.

Some are perfect, and some twisted
grown around obstructions and dense sediment.
There is nothing as beautiful, as cool and surprising
as pure and promising.
Hold them in your hand, and you feel like weeping.

If, for fear of disappointment, you have brought no box or basket
just collect them into your jumper.
Carry them inside, make a still-life.
God, how clean they are, coming from the chilled dirt
you can hardly believe they are yours.

Collecting Mushrooms

for Miriam Porter

So worn with use, your bent sculptor's hands
prise these up from pine needles and cold Autumn wetness.
No leaf's red could match the colour of your hair
and you with your basket
knowing all the names
smelling of sandalwood,
you are my good and benign rural witch.
Back at your house, this fluted golden harvest
spreads around us like a meteorite shower.
You mix tamari, seasalt, pinenuts
and these mushrooms, still smelling like crumbling forest,
into an elixir of sesame oil,
humming like a careless alchemist.

Later I will thread a basketful in front of the fire
and feel that same forager's surge of contentment
that sound they made,
tearing from the earth, creamy and miraculous
like the wood sighing as it warms
like an exhaled breath as you rise and brush your knees.
My mouth tastes each satisfying vowel and consonant,
delicious with something scarce made abundant:
Saffron Milkcaps
there's not one thing about that name I don't like.

We have been too wise for the gleaming cosmetics counter,
Seeing straight through the pseudo-science glamour –
None of us want acrylic nails, or believe for one second
that a model in a white coat and glossy hair
is leaning over a petri dish in the Pond's Laboratory on our behalf
opening her glossy mouth with amazement at a breakthrough.

It is the potions that fell us, here in the home straight;
with plausible stories of toxins we've unwittingly accumulated
and need to be cleansed of
inescapable impurities that are stored just beneath the skin
robbing us of what we deserve,
knobbly handcut soaps filled with chunks of purifying seaweed,
woody fragrances stored in the holds of spice voyagers
and someone younger than us assuring us it's made by hand
with no impurities, no detergents, no artifice
some handed-down medieval wisdom
distilled from nettle and witch-hazel.

We fall for it every time, us second-wave women.
The mystique of the potions,
the idea that what we have inherited and absorbed can be foamed away
that a soothing astringent will cool our smothered rage
that there is a new surface, waiting to be revealed
beneath the old surface,
that our skin is starving
and must be fed.

We succumb to a fabled island of botanica exotica:
papaya and dewberry, kiwifruit and lime,
crushed pearl and hibiscus
naturally-sourced mineral clay
and gently exfoliating black volcanic sand,

some seductive beach with warm spring breezes,
and us in the middle of it, where we belong,
hair long and waving down our unmarked, cocoa-buttered backs
breathing sandalwood and sweet almond.
See – Cook's sailors are staggering ashore
gobsmacked by lust, as we wait like queens
offering ripe mangoes and avocados,
ready to be nourished and nurtured
and never hunger again

They know just which born-again mantras will nail us:
Replenish reinvigorate revive restore
We pause at the clean-scrubbed bottles
the faux hand-lettered labels
and hear *you deserve it*
you are pure
you are essential
and get out our wallets, to pay again.

This needle heated green then orange over the gas ring
has tempered itself to black now
the woodcarver's palm is still and heavy
lying like a curled shingle in my own.

I smooth the fingers out flat
and find the barb against skin dense with calluses
a jagged root buried crosswise against the grain
solid as an old fencepost sunk in a ploughed field

I am not digging into flinching flesh
the woodcarver looks thoughtfully out the window as I probe
I become a small toiling figure
my needle a dwarf axe, a marvel of the Bronze Age
the ground is hard
dry creekbeds branch from me in all directions
four ridges pillow on the horizon
under my feet run blue seams of coal.

I prise it clear, levering and uprooting,
no blood from that weathered palm, polished smooth with use,
and as I sit back breathing again
the woodcarver turns and laughs;
Finished already? I didn't feel a thing.

On the windows in the room
you slept in as a boy
there is wire netting but no glass

I imagine you shivering
turning your small back to the cold.

Your brother says
he banished you from the room you shared
because the sound of you
singing yourself to sleep each night
drove him crazy.

You say you chose to go
both of you laugh, now,
sip your beers.

But I see you have mastered
the austerity of self-preservation.
You comfort yourself
by curling away
endurance you learned
in the long hours waiting for morning
alone in the sun room.

I will lay both my hands
on those resisting arms.
I will learn
the lyrics to that song.

A breeze stirs them
folds hot stunned air
into these dull resonances
flat as a stick against a wooden fence
dragged on the reluctant journey home.

Motionless, I am poised here
listening to the pitched clack of dry bamboo,
like skeletons and beaks of birds
too cumbersome to survive,
fingers listlessly sifting through shells,
or how my own long hollow bones would sound
tempered, and emptied
after walking miles to get
exactly here

Is it that I can tolerate having no name for this
or is it just that I am getting better
at hearing
the emptiness
inside things

my palms open
the wind
bending careless around me

I am being told a long story of a chain of coincidences.
A friend, losing her way in the desert
walks out of a dry Alice Springs riverbed into thirty thousand miles
of flat ruled horizon, blazing heat, waterless saltbush.
She finds a fence and walks along it

A sign tells her she has reached a rifle range
and, in the distance, the mirage shimmer of a tin shed.
She is thirsty, and she trespasses
climbs through the fence
walks expecting rifle fire
forces the door.

In the dimness she finds nothing but a big empty crate
and abandoned, waiting silence.
She has one chance, and she sees it.
She takes the crate outside, stands it on end, climbs it,
and pulls herself onto the roof of the shed.
Turning in a slow 360 degrees she catches sight
of the low mountain range she recognises as north,
elevated over the line of the horizon
the direction back to town
sets off, swallowing dust
weak with relief.

The point of the story is yet to come – the birth of her daughter
brought about by a lift, once she found the road back to town,
from a stranger she flagged down, and so forth –
I listen, but part of my mind
stays lingering in the gloom with that crate
and her presence of mind, stilling panic
recognising it for what it was.

I wonder how many times I have broken some lock
searched hastily and withdrawn
thinking the room empty,
overlooked the disguised and waiting gift
missed the mountain.

I wonder what my stunted sightline
has failed to notice
what path home
I have abandoned.

The moment will come, next year or else today
No-one talks about it, but it's true:
Grief is work – implacable, in our way
a snarled, exhausting thing we need to do.

It waits for us. We'd rather it grew weeds
like a burnt down house, or rusted wreck,
than see its scalded bulk beneath the reeds
and haul its wreckage up onto the deck.

And grief is like Pompeii, each shard a clue
to be painfully recovered on our knees
No-one talks about it, but it's true
we must kneel down and name it piece by piece.

We falter at the task that lies at hand
the hard-won pattern we must pick apart
the broken glass that we must sift like sand
the knives we turn on our constricted heart

and all the bloodless scars we hoped to leave –
we do not get to shirk, or even choose
to see the world the way we would believe.
This world which uses us. This world we use.

Love and work, Freud tells us, is the cure
but love, this tapped vein that has bled too much,
has left us just with work, and now I fear
the toxic half-life of this thing still warm to touch.

Darkness hides the waiting shapes of day
that will lie there till we steel ourselves to start.
Here comes the light. We cannot turn away;
Seeing is the hardest but most necessary part.

We are crouched in do-it-yourself land
arguing over preparation and degrees of finish
rolling brickie's sand smooth as a piecrust.

The pattern is a simple herringbone
these bricks are salvaged
they have all been handled and rehandled
we are saving ourselves thirty dollars an hour
to learn the hard way about warp and imperfection.

We graze our hands, raise calluses, crawl like penitents
this pattern veers
away from right-angles
you can't cut them to fit, they are fired that way –
adjust your string-lines
adjust them, or shut up.

We have stopped talking.
Your mouth makes its odd line
as you smack the lines I've laid
with the rubber mallet.
We only have one of these
we must take it in turns
to impose our versions of what's correct.

We cross each other's shadows,
yearning for the soft sand and the broom
that sweet curve disappearing around the corner,
soft groundcovers hiding our errors.
You stretch your spine, melancholy with your own thoughts,
I suck a blood blister raised by the nip of cruel stone
we knock off mortar with chisels
the rasping echoes like throat-clearing.

We will invite others to walk on this
as if making it was effortless.
I crawl forward brick by misshapen brick
already knowing this
already forgiving us
our small and fallible trespasses.

Edged in silver nitrate like a negative
red river gums throw arms up into the sky
the garden lies buried under a sea of leaves

I stand resting my palm
on a cool wall I rendered and painted myself
I feel the velvety burr of limewash, its calcium shell
my heartbeat repeats: *my hand has made this*
that sound in my ear like a tide.
I remember discarding the shredding gloves,
that grit and slide of mud
I could have rendered the whole house, hard and smooth
and finished without fingerprints, without skin
I fit my palm to it gently now, for comfort.

It's 4 a.m, and the river, invisible down there,
is a sleeping mouth poured full of mist.
I will hear the night train soon, tinny in the cold
iron tracks stretching before it like a ladder
bed waiting upstairs like a whale's belly.

The night will overbalance then, and spill,
draining around fogged-glass monochrome,
icebergs drifting somewhere
this wall glowing like nacre
and a pale moon risen like a fine white scar.

My right hand floats out
to greet everything –
the curving hand carved on the stone knee
of the Egyptian temple god on exhibit
at the Metropolitan Museum in New York,
the perfect lintel over the door of an oratory,
its stones fitted together like teeth,
the letters of the first Celtic alphabet on a stone
barely there now, eroded into air and words.

3,000 years, 1200 years, 800 – it all melts away,
their hand holding the chisel and my hand empty
our fingers closing together on this,
this offering, this love letter, this moment, this marvel.
I greet
all these labours of love
all these hands moving
synchronous
in sign language
through mediums more durable than one lifetime.

Our fingertips touch
through chilled stone,
the church a ruin, the museum
guarded with lasers.
We call our greetings and farewells
we call thankyou, outstretched and faint
yearning across darkness like an empty field
lowering our arms finally,
and turning back, treading blindly
towards the window-lit house
the unimaginable future.